ANIMAL dictionary

make believe ideas

a b c d e f g h i j k l m n o p q r s t u v w x y z

Aa

albatross

An **albatross** is a big seabird that spends most of its life in the air.

amphibian

Amphibians begin life under water, but change as they grow so they can breathe air and live on land, too.

animal

An **animal** is something that lives and moves around. Eagles, goldfish, spiders and rabbits are all animals.

angelfish

Colourful **angelfish** often live in warm seas. Their flat bodies make it hard for enemies to see them from the front.

ant

Ants are tiny insects that live together in big groups called colonies.

alligator

Alligators are reptiles that live in swamps and have long tails, short legs and fierce snapping jaws.

antelope

Antelopes are deer-like animals with horns on their heads.

2

antennae

Lots of insects have two **antennae** on their heads to help them smell and taste.

antenna

antler

The horns on a male deer's head are called **antlers**.

antler

Bb

baboon

Baboons are monkeys that live in big groups. They sleep sitting upright to be alert for danger.

bat

A **bat** is a small, furry night-time animal that looks like a mouse with wings. Bats hang upside down when they sleep.

ape

An **ape** looks like a monkey but has no tail.

badger

Badgers are night-time animals that eat small animals, fruit and worms.

beak

A **beak** is the hard part of a bird's mouth.

beak

a b c d e f g h i j k l m n o p q r s t u v w x y z

bear

A **bear** is a big, heavy animal with thick fur and sharp claws. Bears sleep for most of the winter.

beetle

A **beetle** is an insect with hard, shiny wing covers. Ladybirds are beetles.

bird

A **bird** has feathers, wings and a beak. Most birds can fly.

bison

Giant American **bison** live in herds on the grasslands of North America. Their thick, shaggy coats keep out the winter cold.

beaver

Beavers live in lakes and rivers and are good swimmers. They build dams in streams to make their homes.

bee

A **bee** is an insect with wings and a sting. Bees make honey.

bill

A bird uses its **bill** to eat, build a nest and smooth its feathers.

bill

4

boa constrictor

A **boa constrictor** is a long snake that winds itself around its prey to squeeze it to death.

Cc

budgerigar

Budgerigars are small birds that live in big flocks in the wild. People often keep budgies as pets.

bull

A **bull** is the male animal of the cow family. Most bulls have horns.

calf

A **calf** is a young cow or bull. Calves drink milk for the first few months of life.

butterfly

A **butterfly** is an insect with four large wings.

camel

A **camel** is an animal with one or two humps on its back.

buffalo

Buffalo are large, cow-like animals that live in groups called herds. They have big horns.

a
b
c
d
e
f
g
h
i
j
k
l
m
n
o
p
q
r
s
t
u
v
w
x
y
z

camouflage

Camouflage is when an animal hides from danger by blending in with the things around it.

cattle

Cows, buffalo and oxen are all kinds of **cattle**.

caribou

Caribou is the North American name for reindeer. Caribou have antlers and live near the icy North Pole.

cat

A **cat** is an animal with soft fur, sharp claws and a long tail. People keep small cats as pets. Lions and tigers are big cats.

centipede

A **centipede** is a creature with lots of tiny legs.

chameleon

A **chameleon** is a lizard that lives in trees. Chameleons can change colour.

caterpillar

A **caterpillar** looks like a worm with legs. It turns into a butterfly or moth.

cheetah

Cheetahs are big, wild cats with spotty coats. They are the fastest runners in the world.

chick

A **chick** is a baby bird.

chimpanzee

Chimpanzees are apes that live in big family groups. They eat and sleep in trees.

claw

A **claw** is a sharp, curved nail on the foot of an animal.

cobra

A **cobra** is a kind of snake with venomous fangs. Its bite can kill.

chicken

A **chicken** is a farm bird. A male is a cockerel and a female is a hen.

chipmunk

Chipmunks are small, stripy squirrels. They have bushy tails and eat nuts.

cockerel

A **cockerel**, or rooster, is a male chicken.

cow

A **cow** is a large female farm animal that produces milk.

crab

Most **crabs** live in or near water. A crab has a hard shell, eyes on stalks and big claws.

crocodile

A **crocodile** is a reptile with sharp teeth, short legs and a long tail.

cockle

A **cockle** is a kind of shellfish that has two fan-like shells joined together.

coyote

Also called prairie wolves, **coyotes** live on the dry, grassy American plains.

coral

Corals are made up of tiny sea creatures. When a coral dies, it can leave a hard skeleton behind.

cub

Young lions, tigers, foxes and bears are called **cubs**.

8

Dd

dog

A **dog** is an animal that barks. Dogs are often kept as pets. Foxes, jackals and wolves are wild dogs.

deer

Deer are shy animals that can run very fast. Male deer, called stags, have branched horns, or antlers. Female deer are called does and babies are fawns.

dolphin

Dolphins are sea mammals. A dolphin has to hold its breath under water.

donkey

A **donkey** is a kind of small horse with long ears. Donkeys are used to carry people and things over rough paths.

dingo

A **dingo** is a wild dog from Australia.

a b c d e f g h i j k l m n o p q r s t u v w x y z

dragonfly

A **dragonfly** is a big flying insect that lives near water.

Ee

eel

An **eel** is a long, slimy, snake-like fish.

duck

A **duck** is a water bird. Ducks have waterproof feathers and webbed feet for swimming.

eagle

An **eagle** is a large bird with big wings, a curved beak and sharp claws for catching its prey.

egg

Birds, fish, snakes, and lizards live inside **eggs** until they are big enough to hatch.

duckling

A **duckling** is a young duck.

elephant

An **elephant** is a large, grey animal with big ears and a long trunk.

ears

Many animals have two **ears** on the top or sides of their heads for hearing sounds.

elephant seal

Elephant seals live in the freezing ocean near the South Pole.

elk

Also called red deer, **elk** live in American forests and have huge antlers.

eye

Animals have **eyes** to see with. Most animals have two eyes, but some, like spiders, can have as many as eight!

feather

A bird has **feathers** on its body to keep it warm and dry. Wing feathers also help birds to fly.

fish

A **fish** is a scaly animal that lives in water. Fish have gills so that they can "breathe" under water.

flamingo

A **flamingo** is a tall, pink bird with very long legs for wading in water at the edge of lakes.

flock

A **flock** is a group of birds or sheep.

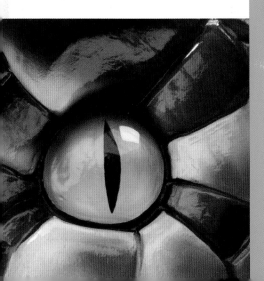

a b c d e f g h i j k l m n o p q r s t u v w x y z

fly

A **fly** is a small insect with one pair of wings. There are lots of different kinds of fly.

frog

A **frog** is a small amphibian that lives in ponds and damp places. Some frogs live high in the treetops.

foal

A **foal** is a young horse. Foals can stand up as soon as they are born. Young zebras and donkeys are also called foals.

fur

Fur is the thick, soft hair that covers some animals.

gazelle

Gazelles are long-legged antelopes that can run fast. They live in big herds on the grasslands of Africa.

fox

A **fox** is a kind of wild dog with a long, bushy tail. Foxes hunt mainly at night.

gerbil

A **gerbil** is a small animal with long back legs and very soft fur.

gibbon

Gibbons are small apes. They use their long arms to swing through trees.

goat

Goats have long hair and horns.

gills

Gills are flaps of skin behind a fish's eye that let it "breathe" under water.

gill

giraffe

A giraffe is a tall animal with long legs and a very long neck.

goldfish

A goldfish is a small, golden-orange fish. People often keep goldfish as pets.

goose

A goose is a large water bird. A male goose is a gander and a baby is a gosling.

13

a b c d e f g h i j k l m n o p q r s t u v w x y z

gorilla

A **gorilla** is a strong ape with long arms for swinging in trees.

guinea pig

A **guinea pig** is a small, furry animal with short legs and no tail.

Hh

gull

Gulls are big birds that usually live near the sea. A gull can catch fish with its long beak.

hamster

A **hamster** is a small, furry animal with pockets inside its cheeks where it can store food.

gosling

A **gosling** is a young goose.

hare

A **hare** is like a big rabbit, with strong back legs and long ears. Hares can run very fast.

grasshopper

Grasshoppers are insects with strong back legs for jumping. They rub their back legs together to make loud noises.

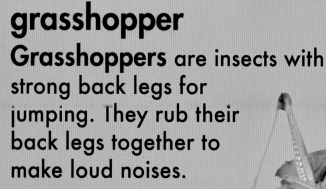

14

hawk

A **hawk** is a bird of prey with sharp claws and a curved, pointed beak for catching and eating meat.

hippopotamus

A **hippopotamus** is a big animal that wallows in the muddy lakes and rivers of Africa.

hedgehog

Hedgehogs are small, spiny night-time animals. When a hedgehog is scared, it rolls into a ball.

heron

Herons are large birds that live near rivers and lakes. They have long legs for wading, and sharp beaks for catching fish.

hoof

A **hoof** is the hard part of a horse's foot. Pigs and deer also have hooves.

hen

A **hen** is a female chicken. Hens lay eggs.

herd

A **herd** is a big group of animals, such as zebras, buffalo, cows or deer.

A
B
C
D
E
F
G
H
I
J
K
L
M
N
O
P
Q
R
S
T
U
V
W
X
Y
Z

horn

horse

A **horse** is a big animal with hooves. People ride horses and use them to pull heavy loads. Zebras and donkeys are kinds of horse.

horn

Rhinoceros, cattle and antelope have hollow **horns** for fighting other animals.

hornbill

A **hornbill** is a bird with a big bill that has a kind of horn on top.

human

A **human** is a man, woman or child.

hyena

Hyenas are dog-like meat eaters that usually hunt at night.

hummingbird

A **hummingbird** is a tiny bird that sips sweet flower nectar through a long, pointed beak. It can hover in the air and even fly backwards.

Ii

iguana

An **iguana** is a large lizard that lives in trees in hot countries.

insect

An **insect** is a small animal with six legs. Many insects have wings. Ants, beetles, butterflies and bees are all insects.

Jj

jaguar

A **jaguar's** spotty coat helps it hide from its prey in the forest.

jellyfish

Jellyfish are soft sea creatures with no bones and stinging tentacles.

Kk

kangaroo

Kangaroos are big, Australian animals with strong back legs for jumping.

kid

A **kid** is a young goat. Children are often called kids, too.

A B C D E F G H I J K L M N O P Q R S T U V W X Y Z

kitten

A **kitten** is a young cat.

ladybird

A **ladybird** is a small flying beetle. Most ladybirds are red with black spots.

lemur

Lemurs live in big groups in the forest on the island of Madagascar.

koala

Koalas are animals from Australia that live, eat and sleep in eucalyptus trees. They sleep a lot and feed mostly at night.

lamb

A **lamb** is a young sheep that is still with its mother.

lamb

leg

Most animals need **legs** to get around. Some animals have many legs; some only have two.

leopard

A **leopard** is a big, wild cat with spots on its coat.

limpet

A **limpet** is a shellfish that looks like a tiny Chinese hat. Limpets stick to rocks under the sea.

lobster

Lobsters live on the seafloor. They have eight legs and two sharp claws.

Mm

macaw

A **macaw** is a kind of parrot. It has a strong, hooked beak for cracking open seeds and nuts.

lion

Lions are big, wild cats that live on the African plains.

lizard

A **lizard** is a reptile with a long body, four legs, scaly skin and a long tail.

lynx

A **lynx** is a wild cat with long legs, a short tail and tufted ears.

llama

Llamas are camel-like animals with long fur.

a b c d e f g h i j k l m n o p q r s t u v w x y z

mammal

A **mammal** is an animal that feeds its babies with its own milk. Mammals generally do not lay eggs and many have hair or fur on their bodies. Cats, goats, dolphins and people are all mammals.

millipede

A **millipede** is a creature with lots of tiny legs. Millipede means "a thousand feet".

mane

A **mane** is the long hair that grows on the back of the neck and head of animals like lions and horses.

marsupial

Marsupials are mammals like koalas and kangaroos whose babies are born very young. The baby crawls to a pouch on its mother's tummy where it grows.

mole

Small, velvety **moles** have front feet like shovels for digging tunnels in the ground.

mongoose

A **mongoose** is a small, fast, meat-eating animal that catches insects and lizards.

mare

A **mare** is a female horse.

20

monkey

Monkeys have strong arms and long tails to swing from tree to tree.

mouse

A **mouse** is a small, furry animal with a long tail. Mice have sharp front teeth for gnawing food.

nest

A **nest** is the home that animals such as birds and mice make for their babies.

moose

A **moose** is the biggest kind of deer. Male moose have huge antlers, which they lose every autumn.

newt

Newts are lizard-like amphibians, which means they can breathe both in and out of water.

moth

A **moth** is a night-time insect with four wings. You often see moths fluttering around lights.

mussel

A **mussel** is a kind of shellfish that has two long oval shells that are joined together.

21

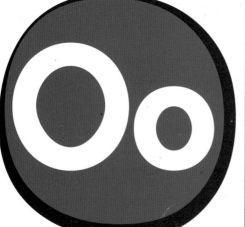

octopus

An **octopus** is a sea animal with a soft body and eight long arms.

ostrich

Ostriches are the world's biggest birds and are bigger than a human. They cannot fly but are very fast runners.

otter

Otters live near water and are very good swimmers with strong, webbed back feet.

owl

An **owl** is a bird that hunts for small animals at night. It has big eyes to help it see in the dark.

orang-utan

Orang-utans are big apes with reddish fur and long arms.

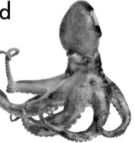

oyster

An **oyster** is a shellfish that has two shells joined together. Pearls grow inside oyster shells.

Pp

parrot

A **parrot** is a bird with brightly coloured feathers and a sharp, curved beak for eating seeds. Some parrots can talk.

pack

A **pack** is a group of dogs or wolves that live and hunt together.

pelican

A **pelican** is a large, fish-eating bird with a big, pouched bill.

panda

Pandas are big, black-and-white bears. They mostly eat shoots of bamboo.

paw

A **paw** is the foot of an animal with claws.

peacock

A **peacock** is a bird. A male peacock can open out its beautiful tail feathers into a shimmering fan.

23

penguin

Penguins are seabirds with black-and-white feathers that mostly live on cold, rocky coastlines. Penguins cannot fly, but they use their wings as flippers to swim.

pony

A **pony** is a small horse.

pheasant

Pheasants are big, brightly coloured birds. They often run rather than fly.

pigeon

A **pigeon** is a bird that makes a cooing sound and lives in woods, towns and cities.

porcupine

A **porcupine** has long spines. If it is attacked, it sticks its spines into its enemy.

piglet

A **piglet** is a young pig.

pig

A **pig** is an animal with a fat body, short legs and a short, curly tail.

polar bear

A **polar bear** is a big, white bear that lives on the ice and snow near the North Pole.

predator

A **predator** hunts and kills other animals for food.

puppy

A **puppy** is a young dog. Puppies love to chew things and can get into trouble!

prey

Prey is any animal that is hunted and eaten by another animal.

puma

A **puma** is a big, wild cat. It is also called a cougar, panther or mountain lion.

puffin

A **puffin** is a seabird with a short, curved beak. Puffins build nests in cliffs.

python

A **python** is a kind of snake that squeezes its prey to death.

Rr

rat

Rats look like mice but are bigger. They will eat almost anything.

reindeer

Reindeer have antlers and live in the icy north.

rabbit

Rabbits are small and furry, with long ears and fluffy tails.

rattlesnake

A **rattlesnake** has a rattle on its tail, which it shakes when it is angry.

raccoon

A **raccoon** has a stripy tail and face markings that look like a mask.

reptile

Reptiles have scaly skin and short legs, or no legs at all. Crocodiles, lizards, tortoises and snakes are all reptiles. Most reptiles lay eggs.

ray

A **ray** is a flat fish with a long tail. Some rays flap their fins like wings under water.

rhinoceros

A **rhinoceros** is a big animal with tough, leathery skin and horns on its head.

Ss

salmon

A **salmon** is a kind of fish that lives in the sea but swims up rivers to lay its eggs.

sea lion

Sea lions live by the sea. They swim well but can also walk on land.

shark

A **shark** is a big fish. Many sharks have very sharp teeth and are fierce hunters.

rodent

Rodents have two strong front teeth for gnawing. Beavers, rats, squirrels and hamsters are all rodents.

scorpion

A **scorpion** has eight legs and a deadly sting at the end of its tail.

seal

Seals are sea animals with flippers for swimming. A seal holds its breath to swim under water.

27

sheep

A **sheep** is a farm animal with a thick, woolly coat. Farmers raise sheep for their meat, wool and milk.

spider

A **spider** is a creature with eight legs. Most spiders spin webs to catch insects for food.

shell

A **shell** is a hard covering around an animal that protects its soft body.

slug

A **slug** has no bones and is like a snail with no shell. As slugs move, they leave slimy trails.

shellfish

A **shellfish** is a soft-bodied animal that lives inside a shell. Some shellfish, like scallops, live between two shells.

snail

A **snail** is a small, soft animal that lives inside a spiral shell. It moves slowly and leaves a slimy trail.

sponge

Sponges are sea animals that feed on tiny animals and plants in the water.

skin

Skin is the outer layer of an animal's body, and it can be covered with feathers, hair, fur or scales.

snake

A **snake** is a scaly reptile with a long body and no legs. Some snakes have a deadly bite.

squirrel

Small, furry **squirrels** live in trees. They have bushy tails and eat nuts.

starfish

A **starfish** is a star-shaped animal with five arms that lives in the ocean.

T t

stag

A **stag** is a male deer. Stags have antlers.

stick insect

A **stick insect** is camouflaged to look just like a stick or a leaf. It can even change colour.

tail

An animal's **tail** is the part that grows out from the end of its back.

tail

swan

A **swan** is a large bird with a long, curved neck. Swans live on rivers and lakes.

tapir

Tapirs live in forests. A tapir has a short trunk for tearing leaves off branches.

stallion

A **stallion** is a male horse.

terrapin

A **terrapin** is a small reptile with short legs and a shell on its back. Terrapins live in lakes, rivers and swamps.

toad

A **toad** is a small, frog-like amphibian that lives in ponds and damp places.

tiger

A **tiger** is a big, wild cat with orange fur and black stripes. Wild tigers are rare, but some still live in India and China.

tortoise

A **tortoise** is a slow-moving reptile with short legs and a big shell on its back.

toucan

A **toucan** is a bird with black-and-white feathers and a large bill.

turkey

Turkeys are large birds that nest on the ground. Farmers raise turkeys for their meat.

tree frog

Tree frogs live in trees. Suckers on their feet help them stick to the branches.

turtle

A **turtle** is a reptile that lives in water. It has flippers to swim and a shell on its back.

Uu Vv

Ww

wildebeest
Wildebeest are big antelopes that live in herds on the African plains. They are also called gnus.

udder
Female cattle have **udders** where milk comes out to feed their calves.

udder

walrus
A **walrus** is a fat, wrinkly sea animal. Walruses have whiskers and tusks.

vulture
A **vulture** is a big bird that eats dead animals.

wasp
A **wasp** is a flying insect with a sting. Wasps have bright yellow-and-black stripes to warn enemies away.

wing
A **wing** is the part of an insect or bird that allows it to fly.

wing

whale
A **whale** is a large sea mammal. Unlike a fish, it breathes air through a blowhole on the top of its head.

a
b
c
d
e
f
g
h
i
j
k
l
m
n
o
p
q
r
s
t
u
v
w
x
y
z

wolf

A **wolf** is a kind of wild dog. Wolves live together in big groups called packs.

Yy

Zz

woodpecker

A **woodpecker** has a sharp beak to peck out insects from bark and to make nests in the trunks of trees.

yak

A **yak** is a large, cow-like animal with lots of shaggy hair and long horns.

zebra

A **zebra** looks like a horse with black-and-white stripes. Zebras live in Africa.

worm

A **worm** is a small, soft animal with a long body and no legs. Earthworms live in the ground.

ANIMAL dictionary

Thematic pages

What is an animal?

An **animal** is a living thing that moves around to find food. Birds, insects and reptiles are animals.

Birds

Birds have feathers and wings and lay eggs. Most birds can fly.

toucan

macaw

duck

hen

Insects

Insects are usually small and have six legs. Many insects can fly.

butterfly

beetle

Amphibians

Amphibians begin life under water, but change as they grow, so they can breathe air.

frog

salamander

Reptiles

Reptiles are dry and scaly. Like birds, they lay eggs.

lizard

snake

tortoise

Mammals

Mammals are warm and usually have fur or hair. Mammal mothers make milk to feed their babies.

monkey

Fish

Fish have scales and live and swim under water.

clownfish

regal tang

seahorse

shark

Pets

Lots of people keep animals as **pets**.
Some small pets need to live in a special cage,
but others, like cats and dogs,
share the whole house.

macaw

tortoise

gerbil

rabbits

kitten
A **kitten** is
a young cat.

ear

eye

whiskers

fur

hamster

budgerigar

puppy
A **puppy** is a young dog.

nose

tail

paw

rat

mouse

goldfish

guinea pig

On the farm

Farmers keep animals for their milk, meat, wool or eggs. Horses are used for riding or to pull carts over rough ground.

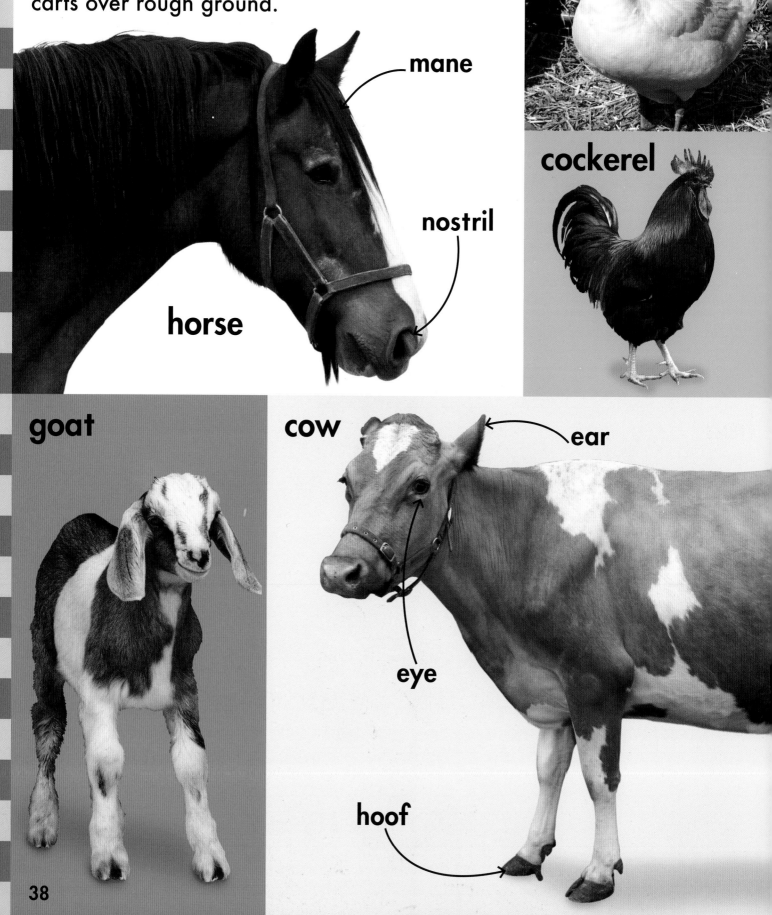

goose

mane

nostril

horse

cockerel

goat

cow

ear

eye

hoof

duck

sheep

turkey

donkey

pig

hen

bull

dog

Parks and gardens

All kinds of animals live in parks and gardens in towns and cities. Some are shy, but others show off!

mole

squirrel

ladybird

peacock

skunk

fluffy tail

white stripe

slug

wasp

pigeon

snail

caterpillar

41

Fields and woods

The woods make a great hiding place for animals and provide plenty of food to eat.

crow

chipmunk

fox

millipede

hedgehog

butterflies

worm

42

woodpecker

deer

tail

leg

moth

mouse

spider

beetle

badger

In the forest

All kinds of animals live in the deep, dark forest. They eat fruits, nuts and leaves, as well as insects and other smaller animals.

raccoon

eagle

hummingbird

bear

fur

nose

leg

sharp claw

porcupine

moose

elk

lynx

wolf

ant

45

Ponds and rivers

Rivers and ponds are full of life. Fish swim in the water, while other animals live on the bank.

salmon

duck

otters

heron

frog

beaver

dragonflies

newt

eye

toe

back

tail

47

Lakes and swamps

Many animals enjoy life in or around lakes. Swamps give crocodiles and hippos a place to hide!

toad

pelican

crocodile

scaly skin

claw

sharp teeth

goose

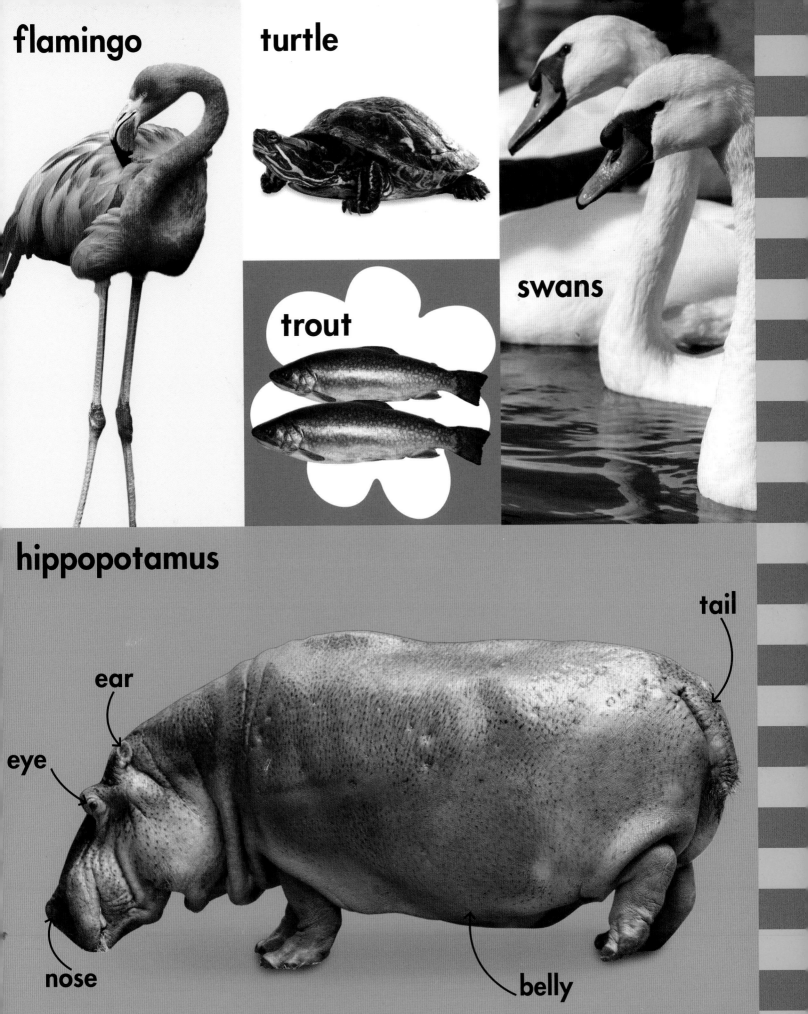

flamingo

turtle

trout

swans

hippopotamus

tail

ear

eye

nose

belly

49

Cliffs and seashores

The beach and high rocky cliffs are home to animals like seals, seabirds and crabs.

mussel

seagull

sea lion

eye

fur

sea anemone

crab

sea urchins

50

cockleshells

starfish

arm

puffin

walrus

waterproof
fur

tusk

In the ocean

The deep waters of the ocean are full of fish of all colours and sizes. But there are many other interesting animals, too.

angelfish

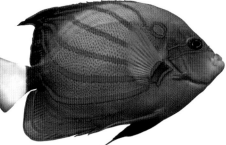

seahorse

eel

dolphin

jellyfish

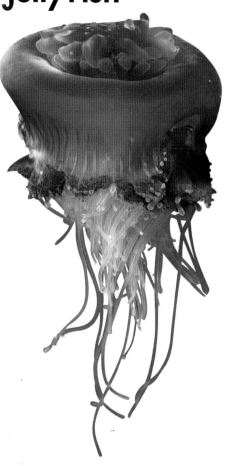

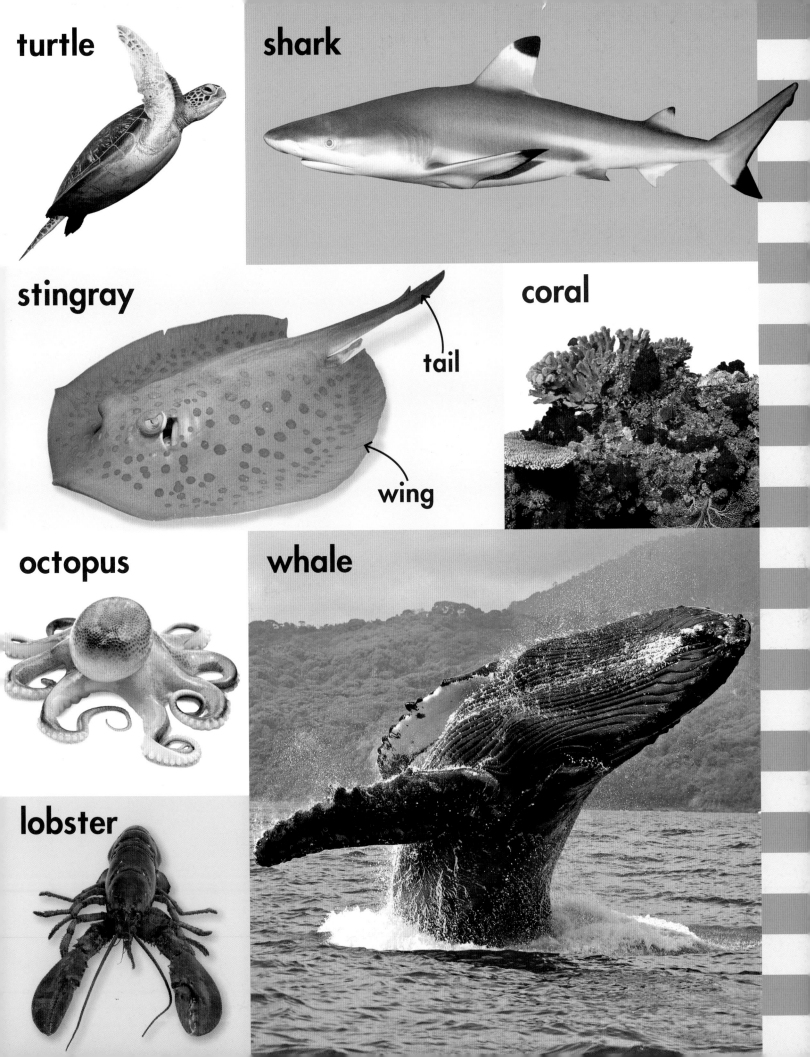

turtle

shark

stingray

tail

coral

wing

octopus

whale

lobster

On the plains

Lots of animals live on wide, grassy plains. Some eat grass and leaves, while others hunt and kill other animals for food. **vulture**

bison

baboon

wildebeest

grasshopper

leopard

lion

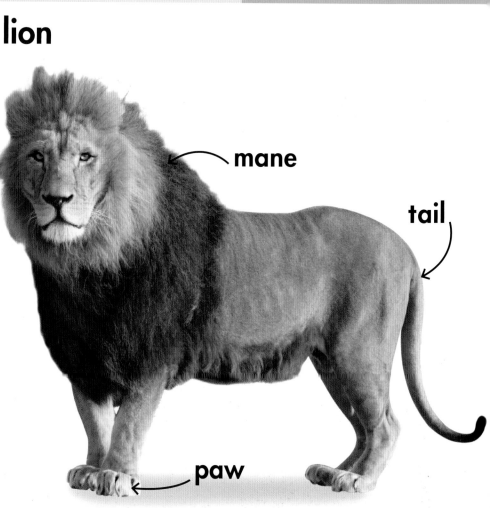

mane

tail

paw

elephant

ear

trunk

leg

zebra

antelope

giraffe

rhino

In the rainforest

The hot rainforest is home to many animals. Some live high in the trees, while others stay on the ground.

tree snake

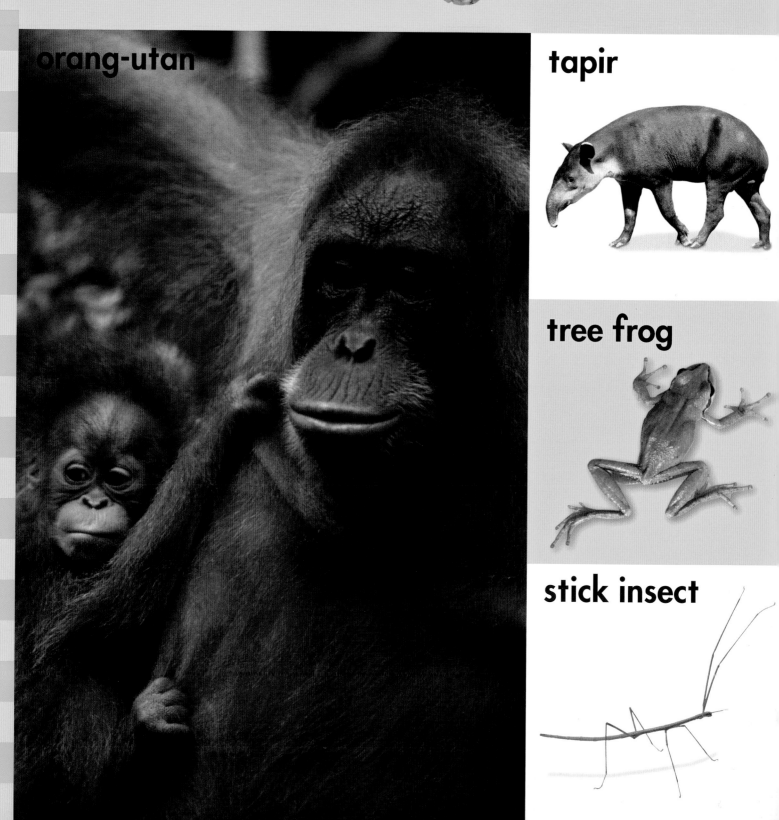

orang-utan

tapir

tree frog

stick insect

parrot

tiger

chameleon

chimpanzee

toucan

gorilla

hornbill

57

Hot and dry

Some animals are able to live in very hot and dry places. Many rest in the shade during the day and come out at night when it is cooler.

rattlesnake

lizard

ostrich

beak

feathers

camel

hump

strong leg

kangaroo

koala

scorpion

strong tail

powerful
leg

mongoose

cheetah

spotty coat

coyote

Mountains, snow and ice

Thick, shaggy fur and plenty of fat helps animals keep warm in the snow and ice of the world's coldest places.

yak

walrus

puma

reindeer

panda

polar bear

white fur

albatross

penguins

seal

llama

Animal babies

Baby animals often have different names than their parents. A kitten is a baby cat or rabbit, and a kid is a baby goat or child!

chicks

piglet

cub

gosling

kitten
ear

tail

duckling

paw

lamb

woolly
coat

kid

foal

puppy

fawn

63